Carnage

EXT. PLAYGROUND IN PARK - DAY

WIDE ANGLE VIEW: A playground in Brooklyn. A winter sun shines brightly. Stark trees and patchy grass.

A boy of about 10 years stands apart from a group of kids his age.

In his hand he is holding a large piece of tree branch, twirling it absently, with the thick end out, for his own amusement.

Another boy, with the support of the group, starts shouting abuse at him. Though the words aren't audible, it's clear that things are getting tense.

A verbal exchange is followed by some threatening gestures on both sides. One boy shoves, the other shoves back.

It's all pretty unremarkable until the first boy, practically reflexively, strikes the second with the branch.

The wounded child is doubled over, his face in his hands.

The others crowd around him.

The boy who hit him also starts to take a step toward the group of children. He seems distraught.

INT. LONGSTREET APARTMENT - DEN - DAY

A narrow room converted to a home office. Winter light filters through the only window.

On a table against one wall there are some periodicals - topical magazines about contemporary history and UNESCO publications. There are also some assorted papers, a school notebook, a few baubles and a laptop computer.

PENELOPE LONGSTREET is seated at the computer.

Her husband, MICHAEL, is standing by amiably, leaning over and already prepared for the words which are to follow.

Also standing there, but a couple of steps back, are ALAN and NANCY COWAN. They are dressed in business clothes. She must have put her coat down somewhere, he has his on his arm. They both stare at the screen.

It is clear from the start that these two couples are not close. The prevailing mood is serious, cordial and tolerant.

PENELOPE reads out loud the words written on the screen:

PENELOPE
"January 11, at 2:30 PM."
(with a glance behind her toward the

COWANS:)
You'll make your statement separately, this is ours.
"...following a verbal dispute in
Brooklyn Bridge Park, Zachary Cowan, age eleven and armed with a stick, struck our son, Ethan Longstreet, in the face. In addition to the swelling and bruising of Ethan's upper lip, this act also resulted in two broken incisors, including nerve damage to the right incisor."

ALAN
Armed?

PENELOPE
Armed. You don't like armed? Michael, what could we say? Carrying? Holding? Carrying a stick, is that all right?

ALAN
Carrying, yeah.

MICHAEL
Carrying a stick.
PENELOPE enters the correction on the laptop.

PENELOPE
Carrying.
She prints the single page and hands it to NANCY COWAN.

PENELOPE (CONT'D)
It's ironic, we always thought the Brooklyn Bridge Park was safe. Compared to Hillside.

MICHAEL
True.
Once the paper is in his wife's hand, ALAN COWAN tries to cut the meeting short, starts backing up toward the foyer.
They continue talking as all make their way progressively toward the front door.

MICHAEL (CONT'D)
We always said, Brooklyn Bridge Park, fine. Hillside, no way.

PENELOPE
Only goes to show you. But hey, thank you for coming. It's so much better than getting caught up in that adversarial mindset.

NANCY
Well we thank you. Really.

PENELOPE
I don't think we have to thank each other. At least some of us still have a sense of community, right?

ALAN
Though the kids haven't got that notion straight yet. I mean our kid.

NANCY
Right, our kid!
Nancy walks into the living room to retrieve her coat.

INT. LONGSTREET LIVING ROOM - DAY
The LONGSTREET's living room is modest and homey. There's a partial view of the elevated subway. The furnishings are improvised and disparate, with a few ethnic touches. There is a large bookshelf.
A few chairs and a sofa are arranged around a coffee table, covered with art books.
There is a large bouquet of tulips in a transparent vase.

NANCY
Those tulips are gorgeous.

PENELOPE
It's that little florist way up on
Henry, you know? The one all the way up.

NANCY
Oh right.

PENELOPE
They fly the bulbs in straight from Holland, twenty dollars a load.

NANCY
That a fact?

PENELOPE
You know the one? All the way up.

NANCY
Right, right.
The COWANS drift toward the foyer, followed closely by the LONGSTREETS.

NANCY (CONT'D)
What about the tooth with the damaged nerve?

PENELOPE
Oh. Well they don't know. There's still some question about the prognosis. Apparently, the nerve is not completely exposed.

MICHAEL
Only part of it is exposed.

PENELOPE
Right. There's a part that's exposed and a part that's still protected. So for right now, they're not going to devitalize it.

MICHAEL
They want to give the tooth a chance.

PENELOPE
We would so like to avoid root canal.

NANCY
Of course.

PENELOPE
So there's an observation period while they give the nerve a chance to heal.

MICHAEL
Meantime, he's going to need caps.

PENELOPE
You can't have implants until you're eighteen.

MICHAEL
You can't.

PENELOPE
The permanent implants can only be done once you stop growing.

NANCY
Naturally. I hope... I hope it all turns out all right.

PENELOPE
We can only hope.
A slightly uncomfortable beat.

PENELOPE (CONT'D)
You know, he didn't want to tell on
Zachary.

MICHAEL
No, he didn't want to.

PENELOPE
I mean it was incredible to see this child with no face left, no teeth. And he just wouldn't talk.

NANCY
I can just imagine.

MICHAEL
He didn't want to tell on the kid. Like his friends would say he was a snitch. I mean let's be honest, Penelope, it wasn't only a sense of honor.

PENELOPE
You could say that. But a sense of honor requires a social context.

NANCY
Naturally. So how did you..? I mean, how did you finally get Zachary's name?

PENELOPE
Well because we explained to Ethan that protecting this child was not going to help him.

MICHAEL
We told him, if this kid thinks he can go on hitting people and getting away with it, why should he stop?

PENELOPE
We told him that if we were that child's parents, we would absolutely want to know about this.

NANCY
Of course.

ALAN
Yeah.
ALAN's cell phone vibrates. He quickly pulls it out of his jacket pocket.

ALAN (CONT'D)
Excuse me one second.
ALAN walks away from the others. While he speaks, he takes a newspaper out of the pocket of his overcoat.

ALAN (CONT'D)
Yes Walter, thanks for getting back to me. So it's in this morning's Journal. I'll read it to you. "According to a study published by British journal
Lancet, two Australian researchers have identified neurological side effects of TW Pharma's anti- hypertension medication Antril, including impaired hearing and muscle coordination, and ataxia."

WALTER (O.S. - TEL)
Fucking hell. How come nobody told me about this?

ALAN
Who the hell does your press monitoring over there?

WALTER (O.S. - TEL)
This is going to be trouble.

ALAN
Yeah, you're in deep shit.

WALTER (O.S. - TEL)
So what do we do? Do we respond right away?

ALAN
No, my problem is the A.S.M. You have an Annual Stockholders
Meeting in two weeks. Did you schedule a contingency for litigation?

WALTER (O.S. - TEL)
I'm not sure, I'll have to check.

ALAN
OK. And Walter, Walter. Talk to PR and find out if it was picked up anywhere else.

WALTER (O.S. - TEL)

Right, right.

ALAN
And call me back.
(hangs up:)
Sorry.

MICHAEL
So you're like a...

ALAN
An attorney.

NANCY
And yourself?

MICHAEL
Houseware supply. Penelope is a writer and she works part time in a bookstore, mostly art books and history books.

NANCY
A writer?

PENELOPE
I co-wrote a volume about Sabean civilization, working from artifacts recovered when they resumed digs after the Ethiopia-Eritrea conflict. And now I have a book coming out in January about the Darfur tragedy.

NANCY
So you specialize in Africa.

PENELOPE
I'm interested in that part of the world.

NANCY
Do you have any other children?

PENELOPE
One daughter. Courtney is nine. She's very angry at her father right now. He got rid of the hamster last night.

NANCY
You got rid of the hamster?

MICHAEL
Yeah. Made such a racket at night.
Those things sleep during the day.
Ethan was going crazy. He couldn't stand the racket that hamster made. Now, I don't mind telling you, I been wanting to get rid of the thing for the longest time.

(MORE)

MICHAEL (CONT'D)
So I thought, that's it. I took it out and left it in the street.

NANCY
You left it in the street?

MICHAEL
I figured it was a gutter-sewer kind of animal, but no. It was scared out of its wits, out there, on that sidewalk. Truth is, they're not pets and they're not wild. I don't know where they belong. Drop them in a clearing in the woods, they're still not happy. I mean where are you supposed to put them?

NANCY
You just left him outside?

PENELOPE
He did, and then he tried to convince
Courtney that the hamster ran away.
Which, of course, she wasn't buying.

ALAN
And this morning the hamster was gone?

MICHAEL
Gone.

PENELOPE
And you? What kind of work do you do?

NANCY
I'm an investment broker.

PENELOPE
Would it be possible -- and I'm just going to come out and ask you directly -- could Zachary apologize to Ethan?

ALAN
It would be good if they talked.

NANCY
He's got to apologize, Alan. He has to actually say he's sorry.

ALAN
Yeah, I mean sure, probably.

PENELOPE
Well is he sorry?

ALAN
He knows what he did. He didn't realize how serious it was. He's eleven years old.

PENELOPE
Eleven is not a baby.

MICHAEL
It's not an adult either. We didn't ask you, you want some coffee or tea? Is there any cobbler left, Penny? She makes a mean cobbler!

ALAN
You got espresso?

MICHAEL
Yeah.

ALAN
(checking his watch)
I wouldn't mind a cup.

NANCY
A glass of water.

MICHAEL
(to PENELOPE:)
Espresso for me too, babe. And bring the cobbler.
PENELOPE leaves the room. After a short beat:

MICHAEL (CONT'D)
You got to taste this cobbler.
MICHAEL suddenly rises, follows PENELOPE out.

INT. KITCHEN - DAY
In the LONGSTREET kitchen, PENELOPE is busy at the espresso machine. MICHAEL enters.

MICHAEL
Where's the cobbler?
They look around the room. Then PENELOPE opens the refrigerator and takes a cake dish out.

PENELOPE
She put the cobbler in the fridge again! I don't know what language I should speak to her in.
MICHAEL takes out some plates and spoons.

MICHAEL
They're nice, right?

PENELOPE
Do you need to tell everyone I'm a writer?
MICHAEL sets out a tray, including the cobbler.

MICHAEL
You are a writer. You wrote a book.

INT. LIVING ROOM - DAY
In the living room, the COWAN's have changed positions: NANCY is sitting in another seat, as if she had gotten up to look at something in the meantime. ALAN is now seated as well.

NANCY
A very nice couple, admit it.

ALAN
Very.
MICHAEL comes back with the tray.

MICHAEL
A good cobbler isn't easy to make.

NANCY
True.
MICHAEL sets the tray on the coffee table. During the following dialog, he carves out portions on the plates and hands them to his guests.

ALAN
What do you sell?

MICHAEL
Decorative hardware. Door locks, handles, copper fittings. And kitchen equipment, pots and pans...

ALAN
That a good living?

MICHAEL
You know, it's not like we had any banner years or anything. It was tough starting out. But long as I'm out there every morning, with my catalog and my sample case, it's a living. Although the cast iron roasting pans do pick up around the holidays!

ALAN
Yeah.
Beat.

NANCY
When you saw the hamster was terrified, why didn't you bring it home?

MICHAEL

Cause I don't touch them.

NANCY
You put it on the sidewalk.
PENELOPE returns with the coffee.

MICHAEL
It was in the cage. I flipped it over. No way I'm touching those things.

PENELOPE
(to ALAN:)
Sugar?

ALAN
No, no sugar. What kind of cobbler you make?

PENELOPE
Apple and pear.

NANCY
Apple and pear?

PENELOPE
Yeah, it's my own little recipe.
(giggles:)
It's too cold. Shame.

NANCY
Apple and pear, that's new to me.

PENELOPE
Apple and pear is a classic. But there's a trick to it.

NANCY
Really?

PENELOPE
You have to cut the pear thicker than the apple, because the pear cooks faster.

NANCY
Oh, right.

MICHAEL
She's not telling you the real secret.

PENELOPE
Let them taste it.

ALAN

Very good. Very good.

NANCY
Delicious.

PENELOPE
Gingerbread crumbs!

NANCY
Oh my God.

PENELOPE
It's sort of a souped-up Betty Crocker recipe. To be honest, I got the idea from his mother.

ALAN
Gingerbread, fantastic. At least we get a new recipe out of this, huh?

PENELOPE
I wish my son didn't have to lose two teeth in the process.

ALAN
Yeah, of course, that's what I meant.

NANCY
You have a novel way of expressing it.

ALAN
No, hey. I....
His cell vibrates - he checks the display.

ALAN (CONT'D)
I have to take this...
(on phone:)
Yes, Walter.

WALTER (O.S. - TEL)
Here's my question: Can we do a letter-to-the-editor?

ALAN
No. No letters to the editor.
You'll just fan the flames.

WALTER (O.S. - TEL)
We can't just turn a blind eye to this!

ALAN
Was it scheduled?

WALTER (O.S. - TEL)

Well, no.

ALAN
Uh-huh.

WALTER (O.S. - TEL)
We decided to let it go.

ALAN
What are these disorders anyway?
What's ataxia?

WALTER (O.S. - TEL)
Lack of balance, unsteady or jerky gait. But that's if you take the whole bottle!

ALAN
And in normal doses?

WALTER (O.S. - TEL)
Normal doses? Rarely.

ALAN
How long have you known this?

WALTER (O.S. - TEL)
Two years. Two and a half years.

ALAN
And in all that time you haven't recalled it?

WALTER (O.S. - TEL)
You're joking, right? Might as well file for Chapter 13.

ALAN
What are we talking about in revenues?

WALTER (O.S. - TEL)
Somewhere around half a billion

ALAN
Oh. Oh, I see.

WALTER (O.S. - TEL)
I'm going to find out who else knows about this report.

ALAN
OK.
ALAN hangs up and immediately dials another number, all the while gobbling down his cobbler.

NANCY
Alan, we're all waiting for you.

ALAN
Yeah, right. One second.
(on cell:)
Dennis?

DENNIS (O.S. - TEL)
Did you talk to him?

ALAN
They've known about the risks for two and a half years.

DENNIS (O.S. - TEL)
Jesus.

ALAN
An internal report, but no undesirable side-effects are firmly established.

DENNIS (O.S. - TEL)
Appropriate action?

ALAN
No. No precautionary measures and they didn't schedule a reserve. Nothing in the annual report.

DENNIS (O.S. - TEL)
I can't believe it. And what are the symptoms?

ALAN
Lack of balance, jerky gait, the works. Basically, you look like you're drunk.

DENNIS (O.S. - TEL)
(laughter)
ALAN and his assistant have a laugh. He stuffs himself with cobbler, laughing and talking with his mouth full, unabashed.

ALAN
Roughly half a billion in revenues.
(long beat:)
You there?

DENNIS (O.S. - TEL)
What did you advise him to do?

ALAN
Deny.

DENNIS (O.S. - TEL)
Of course.

ALAN
That dumbshit wanted us to write a letter to the editor. No way we're writing a letter. On the other hand, if we see this is getting picked up, we could do a press release. Like somebody's spreading false rumors two weeks out from the A.S.M. kind of thing.

DENNIS (O.S. - TEL)
Want me to broach it with him?

ALAN
He's calling me back.

DENNIS (O.S. - TEL)
All right. We hold tight for now. We work on a press release.

ALAN
OK.
(hangs up)
I've been so busy, I hardly had time for lunch.

MICHAEL
Help yourself, help yourself.

ALAN
Thanks. I know I'm pushing it. Where were we?

PENELOPE
We were saying it would have been better to meet some other way.

ALAN
Oh, right. Yeah. So this cobbler, your mother, huh?

MICHAEL
It's my mother's recipe but Pen made it.

PENELOPE
Your mother's doesn't make it with pear and apple!

MICHAEL
No.

PENELOPE
She has to have an operation, poor thing.

NANCY

Yeah? What for?

PENELOPE
The knee.

MICHAEL
She's going to get a polyethylene and metallic prosthesis. She's wondering what's going to be left of it after the cremation.

PENELOPE
Michael, that's mean.

MICHAEL
She doesn't want to be buried with my father. She wants to be cremated, and put upstate next to her mother, who's all alone. A couple of urns jabbering away on the shores of Lake Sebago. Ha, ha!
Everyone laughs politely. They all rise. Very discreetly, ALAN edges toward the exit.

NANCY
We're very touched by how generous you're being. We realize how you're trying to smooth things out here instead of making them worse.

PENELOPE
Please, it's the least we could do.

MICHAEL
Yeah!

NANCY
No, come on. So many parents just take their kids' side, acting like children themselves.
(MORE)

NANCY (CONT'D)
If Ethan had broken two of Zachary's teeth, I'm thinking Alan and I might have had more of a knee-jerk reaction. I'm not sure we would see the big picture.

MICHAEL
Sure you would!

ALAN
She's right. I'm not so sure.

MICHAEL
You would. Because we all know it could have happened the other way around.
Beat. PENELOPE's disapproval of her husband's remark is silent, but clear.

PENELOPE
So what does Zachary say? How is he experiencing this?

NANCY

He doesn't talk much. A little overwhelmed I guess.

PENELOPE

But he realizes that he disfigured his schoolmate?

ALAN

No. No, he doesn't realize that he disfigured his schoolmate.

NANCY

Why do you say that? Of course
Zachary realizes!

ALAN

He realizes that this violent behavior is unacceptable. Not that he disfigured his schoolmate.

PENELOPE

You don't like the word but unfortunately the word is appropriate.

ALAN

My son did not disfigure your son.

PENELOPE

Your son disfigured our son. Come back after school hours, look at his mouth and teeth.

MICHAEL

Momentarily disfigured.

ALAN

His mouth will be fine when the swelling goes down. As for the teeth, if he needs it, we'd be willing to chip in for the best dental care...

MICHAEL

We got insurance for that. What we want is for the boys to patch it up, make sure nothing like this ever happens again.

NANCY

Let's set up a meeting.

MICHAEL

Yeah. Exactly.

PENELOPE

With us there?

ALAN

They don't need coaching. Let them work it out like men.

NANCY

Like men. Alan, don't be ridiculous. On the other hand, maybe we don't need to be there. Maybe it's better if we weren't there, right?

PENELOPE
The issue is not whether we should be there or not. The issue is, do they want to talk, do they want to clear this up?

MICHAEL
Ethan does.

PENELOPE
But Zachary?

NANCY
We won't give him a choice.

PENELOPE
It has to come from him.

NANCY
Zachary acts like a thug, we're not going to wait around for him to see the light.

PENELOPE
If Zachary sees Ethan in a punitive context, because he's forced to, I can't see anything positive coming out of that.

ALAN
Mrs. Longstreet, our son is a maniac. If you hope he'll suddenly and spontaneously get all apologetic, you're dreaming. Look I'm sorry, but I really do have to get back to the office.
ALAN forces the moment. "Time to go."
NANCY rises as well. Pretty soon, everyone is standing.

INT. FOYER - DAY
ALAN
Nancy, you stay. You'll let me know what was decided. I'm no use to anyone anyway. Women think you need the man, you need the father, like it would do any good.

NANCY
I'm really sorry, but I can't stay either. My husband has never been much of an I'll-push-the-stroller type daddy.
Everyone drifts toward the door.

PENELOPE
Too bad. It's wonderful walking with a child. It goes by so fast. Michael, you really liked taking care of the kids, you had a ball pushing that stroller.

MICHAEL
Yeah, sure.

INT. ELEVATOR & LANDING - DAY
Everyone is in the foyer. PENELOPE hands NANCY her coat and she puts it on. ALAN has opened the door and is already at the doorstep when PENELOPE speaks:

PENELOPE
So what should we decide?

NANCY
Could you come over to our place at about seven-thirty, with Ethan?

PENELOPE
Seven-thirty? What do you think,
Michael?

MICHAEL
Well, if you want my opinion...

NANCY
Yes, please.

MICHAEL
I think Zachary should come over here.

PENELOPE
Yes, I agree.

MICHAEL
The victim shouldn't be the one who makes the trip.

PENELOPE
That's right.
ALAN already has one foot out on the landing.

ALAN
I can't be anywhere at seven-thirty.

NANCY
Who needs you? You're useless, right?

PENELOPE
Seriously, I think it's a good idea for his father to be there.
ALAN's cell vibrates again.

ALAN
(answering PENELOPE:)
All right but not tonight.
(on phone:)
Yeah?
(backing off the elevator:)

Can you hear me now? Hello?

His cell phone stuck to his ear, ALAN uses the moment to step out on the landing and ring for the elevator.

FEMALE ASSOCIATE (O.S. - TEL)
Mr. Cowan? Mr. Cowan? We're looking at the paperwork but we haven't seen the annual report.
Did you see it?

ALAN
There's not a word in the annual report. But the risk wasn't officially established. There's no proof.

FEMALE ASSOCIATE (O.S. - TEL)
OK.
He hangs up.
NANCY is on the landing as well. PENELOPE and MICHAEL quickly amble down the hall toward the elevator.

PENELOPE
How about tomorrow?

ALAN
Tomorrow I'm in Washington.

MICHAEL
You have business in Washington?

ALAN
At the Pentagon.

NANCY
Look, the main thing is to get the kids to talk. I'll come over to your place with Zachary at seven-thirty and we'll let them talk it through. What? You don't seem convinced.

PENELOPE
If Zachary hasn't acquired accountability skills, they'll just glare at each other, it will be a disaster.

ALAN
Accountability skills, Mrs.
Longstreet? What are you talking about?

PENELOPE
I'm sure your son is not a maniac.

NANCY
Zachary is not a maniac.

ALAN
Yes he is.

NANCY
Alan, don't be an idiot. Why are you saying that?

ALAN
He's a maniac.

MICHAEL
How does he explain what he did?

NANCY
He won't talk about it.

PENELOPE
He should talk about it.
The elevator arrives. ALAN holds the door open and puts one foot inside as he speaks.

ALAN
Mrs. Longstreet, that's a lot of "shoulds". He should come here, he should talk about it, he should feel sorry. I'm sure you're much more evolved than we are. We're trying to get up to speed, but in the meantime try to indulge us.

MICHAEL
Hey come on! What happened here? This isn't what we're about.
With friendly authority, MICHAEL claps a hand on ALAN's shoulder and leads him back into the hallway. The elevator door closes.

PENELOPE
I'm talking about him. About Zachary.

ALAN
I got that, yeah.

NANCY
Alan.
NANCY gives her husband a long look.
In the secret language of couples, the single name pronounced and the reproving look get the best of ALAN.
Everyone walks away from the elevator.

MICHAEL
Want some more coffee? Real coffee?

NANCY
Coffee, thank you.
Pause. Michael looks at Alan.

ALAN
Coffee, all right.
PENELOPE has made no signs of going for the coffee.

MICHAEL
It's OK, Pen. I'll get it.

INT. LIVING ROOM - DAY
PENELOPE, NANCY and ALAN are standing in the living room.
They are all very uncomfortable.
Awkward silence.

NANCY
I see you're an art enthusiast.
NANCY leans over and delicately picks up a book featuring the painter, Bacon.

NANCY (CONT'D)
I love Bacon, too.

PENELOPE
Oh yes, Bacon.

NANCY
(leafing through the book:)
Cruelty and splendor.

PENELOPE
Chaos. Balance.

NANCY
Yes...

PENELOPE
Is Zachary interested in art?

NANCY
Not as much as he should be. Your children are?

PENELOPE
We try. We try to make up for the lack in the school curriculum.

NANCY
Right.

PENELOPE
We try to get them to read. Take them to concerts and galleries. I do believe that culture can be a powerful force for peace.

NANCY

You're so right.
MICHAEL comes back with the coffee.

MICHAEL
(as he walks in:)
Is cobbler cake or pie? This is an important question. I was in the kitchen, thinking. Why should Linzer torte be a pie? Go ahead, go ahead, don't leave that miserable little piece.

PENELOPE
Cobbler is cake. If there's no crust on the bottom then it can't be pie.
Taking MICHAEL's lead, they sit down again, clearly not for long - NANCY hasn't even taken her coat off.

ALAN
You're a gourmet chef.

PENELOPE
I like cooking. It's something you have to do out of love or not at all. The way I see it, if there's no crust on the bottom, then it's not pie.

MICHAEL
What about you guys? You have other kids?

ALAN
I have a son by a former marriage.

MICHAEL
I was wondering. I know it's not important but what were they arguing about? Ethan won't say a word on the subject.

NANCY
Ethan wouldn't let Zachary be part of his gang.

PENELOPE
Ethan has a gang?

ALAN
And he called him a snitch.

PENELOPE
(to MICHAEL:)
Did you know that Ethan had a gang?

MICHAEL
No. But I'm thrilled to hear it.

PENELOPE
Why are you thrilled?

MICHAEL
Cause I had one too, I was the leader.

ALAN
So was I.

PENELOPE
What does the leader of a gang do?

MICHAEL
You know, you got five, six guys who like you and they're willing to sacrifice themselves for you. Like in Ivanhoe.

ALAN
Like in Ivanhoe, exactly!

PENELOPE
Who even knows Ivanhoe any more?

ALAN
So it's another role model. Like
Spiderman or whoever.

PENELOPE
Well apparently you know more about it than we do. Zachary wasn't quite as silent as you first said he was. And why did he call him a snitch?
Forget it, silly question. That's a silly question. I mean I don't even care, that's not the point.

NANCY
We're not going to get into these children's quarrels.

PENELOPE
It's none of our business.

NANCY
Right.

PENELOPE
What is our business is this unfortunate incident. Violence is our business.

MICHAEL
When I was the leader, in fifth grade, I beat Jimmy Leach in a fair fight and he was stronger than me.

PENELOPE
What does that mean, Michael? What has that got to do with anything?

MICHAEL
No, nothing.

PENELOPE
We're not talking about a fair fight. These children weren't having a fight.

MICHAEL
Right, right. I was just remembering something.

ALAN
It's not very different.

PENELOPE
Yes it is. Excuse me but there is a difference.

MICHAEL
There is a difference.

ALAN
What difference?

MICHAEL
Jimmy Leach and me, we agreed to fight.

ALAN
Did you mess him up?

MICHAEL
A little, sure.

PENELOPE
All right, enough about Jimmy Leach. Would you mind if I talked to Zachary?

NANCY
Of course not!

PENELOPE
I wouldn't do it without your permission.

NANCY
Talk to him. That's completely fine with us.

ALAN
And good luck with that.

NANCY
Stop it, Alan. I don't understand you.

ALAN
Mrs. Longstreet is acting...

PENELOPE

Penelope. I think we'll do better if we're on a first name basis.

ALAN

Penelope, you're acting on a desire to educate, and I think that's just great...

PENELOPE

If you don't want me to talk to him, I won't.

ALAN

Go ahead and talk to him, lecture him, do whatever you want.

PENELOPE

I don't understand how you feel so uninvolved here.

ALAN

Mrs...

MICHAEL

Penelope.

ALAN

Penelope, I am very involved. My son injured another child...

PENELOPE

Deliberately.

ALAN

See, that's the kind of thing that irks me. We know deliberately.

PENELOPE

But that's what makes all the difference.

ALAN

The difference between what and what? We're only talking about one thing here. Our kid picked up a stick and hit your kid. That's why we're here, right?

NANCY

Fruitless.

MICHAEL

Guys. Right, she's right. This kind of talk is fruitless.

ALAN

Why do you feel you need to slip in the word deliberately? What kind of lesson are you trying to teach me?

NANCY

(suddenly rising:)

All right, this is getting silly. My husband is all stressed out over work stuff. I'll come back here tonight with Zachary and we'll let them work it out naturally.

ALAN
I am not stressed out in the least.

NANCY
Well I am.

MICHAEL
There's no reason to be stressed out.

NANCY
Yes there is.
ALAN's cell vibrates.
He rises and takes a step away, trying to keep his conversation separate.

ALAN
Yeah?
While he speaks on the phone, the others try to continue their own dialog.

WALTER (O.S. - TEL)
OK, it has been picked up. We've got three radio stations after us for comment.

ALAN
No comment.

WALTER (O.S. - TEL)
Well maybe we could just say we're...

ALAN
No. Comment.

WALTER (O.S. - TEL)
What if I say that we're awaiting confirmation and that we would recall it...

ALAN
No, you can't recall it! If you recall it, you're admitting liability!

WALTER (O.S. - TEL)
This whole thing is weighing on me. There are real patients behind this, who...

ALAN
Recalling Antril would be admitting your liability!

PENELOPE
In the school play last Christmas, wasn't it Zachary who played...

NANCY

Ebenezer Scrooge.

ALAN
There's no contingency budgeted in the annual report. I mean if you want to get accused of accounting irregularities, if you want them to haul you out of the meeting in handcuffs two weeks from now, go right ahead and recall it!

PENELOPE
Ebenezer Scrooge, right.
In order to counter the nuisance of the other conversation, ALAN speaks louder and louder into his phone.

WALTER (O.S. - TEL)
My personal responsibility is a factor here. I'm thinking about the victims, the families...

ALAN
Let's think about the victims after the stockholders' meeting, Walter.

WALTER (O.S. - TEL)
Children take Antril!

ALAN
We'll see where the stock is after the meeting.

WALTER (O.S. - TEL)
Well, you're the attorney.
PENELOPE raises her voice as well, to compensate.

PENELOPE
He was wonderful.
NANCY sits down with some difficulty. She doesn't look well.
NANCY
Yes.

ALAN
We can't recall a drug because three guys can't walk a straight line!

WALTER (O.S. - TEL)
Right.

ALAN
For the time being, don't make a move.

WALTER (O.S. - TEL)
All right, all right. I won't do anything without your OK.

ALAN
Good, call you right back.
ALAN hangs up and immediately calls his assistant.

PENELOPE
We remember him as Scrooge. Right
Michael? You remember.

MICHAEL
Sure, sure.

ALAN
(to his assistant:)
They're in panic mode. They have the media breathing down their necks.

PENELOPE
With that night bonnet. He was very funny.

NANCY
Yes.

ALAN
(raising his voice:)
I want a release that doesn't sound defensive at all. Just the opposite. Go for the jugular. TW Pharma is a target. Attempt at manipulation of the stock two weeks before the stockholders' meeting. Where did this study come from anyway? How does this suddenly drop out of a clear blue sky, etcetera. Not one word about the health issue. Only one question: Who is behind the study? Who?

DENNIS (O.S. - TEL)
Got it.

ALAN
Fine.
He hangs up. A short silence.

MICHAEL
Pharmaceutical companies are the worst, right? Profit, profit, profit.
ALAN is hardly listening and answers reflexively, all the while trying to dial another number.

ALAN
Nobody said you should listen to my conversation.

MICHAEL
Nobody said you should have it under my nose.

ALAN
(still elsewhere:)
Wrong. I am totally forced to have it here. Against my will, believe me.

MICHAEL
They just peddle the shit, right?

Nobody's responsible.

ALAN has his cell to his ear. He is speaking to MICHAEL, but obviously waiting for an answer on the phone, which doesn't come.

ALAN
In any therapeutic advance there are benefits and there are risks.

MICHAEL
Yeah, sure I know. Still. I mean you got some funny line of work.
ALAN gives up on his call and comes over to stand in front of MICHAEL.

ALAN
What does that mean?

PENELOPE
Michael, it's none of our business.

MICHAEL
Funny line of work.

ALAN
What about you, what do you do?

MICHAEL
I got a normal job.

ALAN
What's a normal job?

MICHAEL
I told you, I sell pots and pans.

ALAN
And door handles.

MICHAEL
And flush mechanisms. And lot of other stuff.

ALAN
Oh, flush mechanisms. I like that.
That's interesting.

NANCY
Alan.

ALAN
I find that interesting. Flush toilets are interesting.

MICHAEL

Why not?

ALAN
How many different kinds do you have?

MICHAEL
There are two basic kinds. You got your push button and your handle operated.

ALAN
Right, yeah.

MICHAEL
Depends where your water line is.

ALAN
I see.

MICHAEL
It either comes from the side near the top, or it comes from the bottom.

ALAN
Right.

MICHAEL
One of my store managers is an expert. I could introduce you if you want, but you'll have to hump it out to Jamaica, Queens.

ALAN
You seem like you know your business pretty well.

PENELOPE
Do you plan to sanction Zachary in some way? You can continue your plumbing discussion in a more suitable setting.

NANCY
I don't feel well.
NANCY rises, takes off her coat, tries to breathe easy as she walks around the room.

PENELOPE
What's the matter?

ALAN
Oh, you do look pale honey.

MICHAEL
You're all white, yeah.

NANCY
I'm nauseous.

PENELOPE is on the case, quickly concerned.

PENELOPE
Nauseous? I have some Reglan.

NANCY
No. I'll be fine.

PENELOPE
What could we..? Coke. What you need is a Coke.
The words are hardly out and she dashes off to the kitchen.

INT. KITCHEN - DAY
In the kitchen, Peneleope swings the refrigerator door open - no Coke. She opens a pantry closet and finds a six-pack of Coke, tears one out of the plastic.
She opens it as she rushes out.

INT. LIVING ROOM - DAY
PENELOPE comes running back into the living room and hands the can to NANCY.

PENELOPE
(terribly sorry:)
It's not cold.
(to MICHAEL:)
It's not cold!

NANCY
You think?

PENELOPE
Oh yes. Little sips.

NANCY
Thanks.

PENELOPE
(to MICHAEL:)
The Coke was not in the refrigerator!
Meantime, ALAN has discreetly called his office back and is listening to someone on the phone.

FEMALE ASSOCIATE (O.S. - TEL)
He's on another call.

ALAN
Oh.

FEMALE ASSOCIATE (O.S. - TEL)
He'll call you right back.

ALAN
Good. Have him call me back. Tell him right away.
(hangs up)
Is Coke good for that? It's more for diarrhea, isn't it?

PENELOPE
Not only.
(to NANCY:)
Better?

NANCY
I'm fine. Mrs. Longstreet, if we decide to reprimand our child, we'll do it in our own way and on our own terms.

MICHAEL
Absolutely.

PENELOPE
What absolutely, Michael?

MICHAEL
He's their son, they're free to do as they see fit.

PENELOPE
I don't agree.

MICHAEL
You don't agree about what, Penny?

PENELOPE
They're not free.

ALAN
Is that right? Go on.
(cell vibrates:)
Oh, sorry.
(on phone:)
Yeah?

DENNIS (O.S. - TEL)
We're in conference. Mark brought everything over.

ALAN
(to his assistant:)
Great.

DENNIS (O.S. - TEL)
We're writing up a statement.

ALAN
But don't forget, nothing has been proven here, nothing is certain.

DENNIS (O.S. - TEL)
Right, right.

ALAN
Don't fuck this up. If we don't get this right, Walter will be out on his ear in two weeks, and so will we.

NANCY
Enough, Alan! Enough with the cell phone already! The here and now, god dammit!

DENNIS (O.S. - TEL)
You sound busy.

ALAN
Yeah.

DENNIS (O.S. - TEL)
Call you back.

ALAN
Right. Call me back and read it to me.
(hangs up)
What the hell is wrong with you? Screaming at me like that! Dennis heard every word!

NANCY
Good! I'm sick of that fucking cell phone, every minute of every day!

ALAN
Listen Nancy, you should be thanking me for agreeing to come here...

PENELOPE
Really!

NANCY
I'm going to throw up.

ALAN
No, you're not.

NANCY
I am.

MICHAEL
You want to use the bathroom?

NANCY
(to ALAN:)
Nobody's forcing you to stay...

PENELOPE
No, nobody's forcing him to stay.

NANCY
I'm dizzy.

ALAN
Stare at a point in space. Stare at a point in space, Doodle. Hey, you can see the el from here. Cool!

NANCY
Get away from me. Leave me alone.

PENELOPE
She should really go to the bathroom, though.

ALAN
Go to the bathroom. Go to the bathroom if you have to throw up.

MICHAEL
Give her some Reglan.

ALAN
It can't be the cobbler, can it?

PENELOPE
I made it yesterday!
Alan tries to put his arm around Nancy.

NANCY
(to ALAN:)
Don't touch me!

ALAN
Take it easy, Doodle.

MICHAEL
Come on, don't get all bent out of shape over nothing.

NANCY
My husband feels that anything to do with the house, the school, the backyard, is my domain.

ALAN
I do not!

NANCY
You do so. And I can understand why.
It's all so excruciatingly boring.
It's excruciating.

PENELOPE
If it's so excruciating, why do you have children in the first place?

MICHAEL
Maybe Zachary picks up on that lack of interest.

NANCY
What lack of interest?!

MICHAEL
You just said it yourself...
NANCY vomits violently. A sudden, catastrophic regurgitation and part of it gets on ALAN.
The art books on the coffee table are also splashed.

MICHAEL (CONT'D)
Go get a bucket, go get a bucket.
PENELOPE rushes off while MICHAEL holds out the coffee tray, just in case.
NANCY heaves again, but nothing comes out.

ALAN
You should have gone to the bathroom.
Doodle, this is ridiculous.

MICHAEL
Your suit took a hit.

INT. HALLWAY IN LONGSTREET APARTMENT - DAY
PENELOPE opens the broom closet and snatches a mop and pail from within.

PENELOPE
(to herself:)
That stupid bitch!

INT. LIVING ROOM - DAY
PENELOPE very quickly returns with the mop and pail.

PENELOPE
(as she enters the room:)
It couldn't be the cobbler. That much I know.
The pail is passed to NANCY.

MICHAEL
It's not the cobbler, it's nerves.

This is just nerves.

PENELOPE
(to ALAN:)
You want to clean up in the bathroom?
Oh my God, my Kokoschka. Oh no.
NANCY vomits bile into the pail.

MICHAEL
Give her some Reglan.

PENELOPE
Not right away. She couldn't keep anything down right now.

ALAN
Where's the bathroom?

PENELOPE
I'll show you the way.
PENELOPE and ALAN exit.

INT. HALLWAY - DAY
ALAN follows PENELOPE down the hall, past the kitchen and the broom closet and, after a quick turn, they reach the bathroom door. PENELOPE opens it and goes inside first.

INT. BATHROOM - DAY
PENELOPE quickly puts away a couple of personal items.
ALAN enters. He has already removed his jacket and tie and his shirt has been sullied as well. The room is small and they are embarrassingly close to one another. PENELOPE is overheated.
She walks out.
ALAN is alone. He turns the faucet on and starts to wash his jacket.

ALAN
Fuck!

INT. LIVING ROOM - DAY
In the living room, NANCY is still leaning over the pail.
MICHAEL is beside her.

MICHAEL
Like I always say, you can't get over something when you're under it.

NANCY
Uh-huh.

MICHAEL
With me it's the back of my neck.
Gets all blocked up right here.

NANCY
Uh-huh.
She spits up a little more bile.
PENELOPE, as frenetic as ever, comes back with a basin of water and a sponge.

PENELOPE
What do we do about the Kokoschka?

MICHAEL
We can fix it. We'll try Lysol, I guess. Only problem is drying it. Or else with plain water and you put some cologne on there.

PENELOPE
Cologne?

MICHAEL
I got some of that Kronos I never use.

PENELOPE
The paper's going to warp.

MICHAEL
We could blow-dry it, then flatten it out with some other books on top. Or else iron it like dollar bills.

PENELOPE
Oh God.

NANCY
I'll buy you another one.

PENELOPE
There is no other one. It's been out-of-print for years.

NANCY
I'm so sorry.

MICHAEL
We can save it. Let me do this, Pen.
She hands him the basin and the sponge, wrinkling her nose.
MICHAEL starts cleaning the book.

PENELOPE
It's a reprint, from more than twenty years ago, of the catalog from the 1963 show in London.

MICHAEL
Go get the blow-dryer. And the Kouros. It's in the bathroom cabinet with the sheets.

PENELOPE
Her husband is in the bathroom.

MICHAEL
He's not on the can!
She exits and he continues to clean.

MICHAEL (CONT'D)
I got most of it off. Little bit on the Dolgans...

INT. BATHROOM - DAY
A knock on the door. PENELOPE enters.
ALAN is drying his jacket with the hair dryer.
She grabs the Kouros and goes back out.

INT. LIVING ROOM - DAY
MICHAEL is now on all fours, cleaning the vomit off the floor.

PENELOPE
(to NANCY:)
Are you feeling better?

NANCY
Yes.

PENELOPE
(to MICHAEL:)
Should I spray?

MICHAEL
Where's the blow-dryer?

PENELOPE
He's using it.

MICHAEL
We'll wait. We'll put the Kouros on there last.

NANCY
May I use the bathroom, too?

PENELOPE
Of course. Yes, of course, of course.

NANCY
I don't know what to say, I'm so sorry.

INT. HALLWAY - DAY
PENELOPE shows NANCY down the hall.

NANCY enters the bathroom - PENELOPE closes the door behind her.

PENELOPE
Bring the blow dryer, please.

INT. BATHROOM - DAY
In the bathroom, NANCY is seated on the edge of the tub, her arms at her sides.
ALAN, shirtless, is now drying his shirt. His jacket is hanging on a peg above some bathrobes.

ALAN
That was un-fucking-believable, what you did.
NANCY nods, cannot suppress a tiny smile.

ALAN (CONT'D)
Her cobbler is horrible.

NANCY
You stuffed your face!
NANCY rises. ALAN steps back to let her clean her face at the sink.

ALAN
Look at my day! I have to get some food in me some time!

After gargling, NANCY sits back down on the edge of the tub.
ALAN puts his shirt back on.

NANCY
Oh God. What the hell are we doing here?

ALAN
(beat, in utter disbelief:)
I hope you're kidding!

NANCY
Why do you argue with her? We'd have been out of here a long time ago if you didn't bicker over every word.

ALAN
You'd rather I was a sheep, like her husband?

NANCY
You think it was the cobbler?

ALAN
Of course it was! A little warm Coke and bang!

INT. LIVING ROOM - DAY
In the living room, MICHAEL and PENELOPE are finishing the restoration of the books.

PENELOPE
What a freaking nightmare!

MICHAEL
He better watch it, he's got me right on the edge.

PENELOPE
She's horrible too.

MICHAEL
Less.

PENELOPE
She's so fake.

MICHAEL
She doesn't bother me that much.

PENELOPE
They're both horrible. Why do you take their side?
She sprays the tulips.

MICHAEL
I don't take their side. What is that supposed to mean?

PENELOPE
You mitigate. You're trying to reconcile everything.

MICHAEL
I am not!

PENELOPE
You are. You had your gang and you were the leader, and they can do whatever they want with their son. Their son is a threat to homeland security! When a kid is a menace to society it's everybody's business. I can't believe she barfed all over my books!
She sprays the Kokoschka.
MICHAEL holds the Dolgans book so she can spray it, too.

PENELOPE (CONT'D)
When you know you're going to toss your cookies, you take precautions.
MICHAEL holds up the Foujita.

PENELOPE (CONT'D)
(whimpering)
The Foujita!
She sprays everything, including herself.

PENELOPE (CONT'D)

Disgusting.

MICHAEL
I was right on the edge with that toilet flushing shit.

PENELOPE
You were incredible.

MICHAEL
I held my own, right?

PENELOPE
Incredible. Jamaica, Queens was genius.

MICHAEL
Little piece of shit. What does he call her?!

PENELOPE
Doodle.

MICHAEL
Yeah right, Doodle!

PENELOPE
Doodle!
They both laugh out loud as Alan appears, holding the blow dryer.

ALAN
Yes, I call her Doodle.

PENELOPE
Oh, I'm sorry. We didn't mean anything. It's just so easy to make fun of other people's pet names. Like what do we call each other, Michael? I'm sure it's worse!

ALAN
You wanted the blow dryer?

PENELOPE
Thank you.

MICHAEL
Thanks.
(taking the blow- dryer:)
We call each other darjeeling, like the tea. Ask me, that's a lot more embarrassing!
MICHAEL plugs in the dryer and starts trying to dry the books. The blow dryer's electric cord is relatively short - he has to bring the books over to work on them.
PENELOPE smooths the wet pages of the Kokoschka catalog.

MICHAEL (CONT'D)

Smooth it out, smooth it out.
As she smooths out the pages, she raises her voice to be heard over the dryer.

PENELOPE
How is she? Is she better? The poor thing.

ALAN
Better.

PENELOPE
I reacted badly. I'm ashamed of myself.

ALAN
No.

PENELOPE
I rubbed it in, about the catalog. I can't believe I did that.

MICHAEL
Turn the page. Pull it taut. Nice and taut.

ALAN
It's going to tear.

PENELOPE
He's right. Michael, that's enough, it's dry. You get so absurdly attached to these things, you don't even really know why.
MICHAEL closes the catalog and the two of them pile some heavy books on top of it.
MICHAEL dries the Foujita, the Dolgans, etc.

MICHAEL
There! Good as new. So where does
Doodle come from? Yankee Doodle?
Cheese Doodle?

ALAN
No, it's a song from Guys and Dolls that goes, Doodle oodle oodle oo.

MICHAEL
I know that! I know that!
(singing:)
I love you a bushel and a peck, you bet your pretty neck I do. Doodle, oodle, oodle, doodle, oodle, oodle...
Ha, ha! Ours is from our honeymoon in India. I called her darjeeling instead of darling. So stupid.

PENELOPE
Should I maybe go check on her?

MICHAEL
Go ahead, darjeeling.
PENELOPE walks to the door. She bumps into NANCY, on her way back to the living room.

PENELOPE
Oh Nancy! I was getting worried. All better?

NANCY
I think so.

ALAN
If you're not sure, stay away from the coffee table.

NANCY
I left the towel in the bathtub. I didn't know where to put it.

PENELOPE
Perfect.

NANCY
I see you cleaned up. I'm so sorry.

MICHAEL
Everything is just fine. All is well.

PENELOPE
Nancy, I'm sorry. I wasn't really there for you. I was so focused on my Kokoschka.

NANCY
That's all right.

PENELOPE
I reacted very poorly.

NANCY
Please.
Awkward silence.

NANCY (CONT'D)
In the bathroom I was thinking.

PENELOPE
(as nicely as she possibly can:)
Yeah?

NANCY
Maybe we glossed over the... Well I mean...

MICHAEL
What is it, Nancy? What?

NANCY
Name-calling is a kind of abuse.

MICHAEL
Sure.

PENELOPE
Depends.

MICHAEL
Well, it depends.

NANCY
Zachary has never been a violent child. He must have had his reasons.

ALAN
Like getting called a snitch!
His cell phone vibrates.

ALAN (CONT'D)
Excuse me.
He walks away, making apologetic gestures to NANCY.

ALAN (CONT'D)
Yes, Walter.

WALTER (O.S. - TEL)
CNN is inviting me for a panel discussion. What do I do?

ALAN
As long as there are no victims on the panel. No victims. I don't want you sitting down with victims.

WALTER (O.S. - TEL)
And I deny...

ALAN
Deny, deny, deny. And if we have to, we'll sue the Journal.

WALTER (O.S. - TEL)
And the press release?

ALAN
We'll e-mail you the draft of the press release, Walter. I got to go, sorry.
(hangs up)
Call me a snitch, it gets a rise out of me.

MICHAEL
Unless it's true.

ALAN
What?

MICHAEL
I mean if the shoe fits.

NANCY
My son is a snitch?

MICHAEL
Come on, I was joking around.

NANCY
So is yours anyway.

MICHAEL
What do you mean so is ours?

NANCY
He snitched on Zachary.

MICHAEL
We coaxed it out of him!

PENELOPE
We're completely off point here.

NANCY
Maybe you coaxed, but he did snitch on him.

ALAN
Nancy.

NANCY
Nancy what?
(to MICHAEL:)
You think my son is a snitch?

MICHAEL
I don't think anything.

NANCY
Well if you don't think anything then don't say anything. Don't make insinuations.

PENELOPE

Nancy, let's not lose our cool here. I mean Michael and I have gone out of our way to be conciliating and fair-minded...

NANCY
Not so fair-minded.

PENELOPE
Oh really? How's that?

NANCY
Superficially fair-minded.

ALAN
Doodle, I really have to go.

NANCY
So go. Coward.

ALAN
Nancy, right now I'm in danger of losing my most important client. So this caring parent crap and the bickering that goes along with it...

PENELOPE
My son lost two teeth. Two incisors.

ALAN
Right, yeah. I think we got that.

PENELOPE
One of them permanently.

ALAN
He'll get new teeth! Better ones! No one chewed his ear off!

NANCY
It was a mistake not to consider the source of the problem.

PENELOPE
There is no source. There's an eleven-year-old kid who hits people. With a stick!

ALAN
Armed with a stick.

MICHAEL
We took that word out.

ALAN
You took it out because we asked you to.

MICHAEL
We took it out with no argument.

ALAN
A word which deliberately establishes intent and excludes any hint of a misunderstanding. Which excludes childhood.

PENELOPE
I'm not sure I can put up with that tone of voice.

ALAN
We're not quite on the same page, you and I. Right from the start.

PENELOPE
Mr. Cowan, there is nothing so frustrating as being upbraided for something we ourselves admitted was a mistake. The word "armed" wasn't right, we changed it. Although, strictly defined, it certainly applies.

NANCY
Zachary was verbally abused and he reacted. If I'm attacked I defend myself, especially when I'm all alone against a whole gang.

MICHAEL
Well, you've certainly perked up since you tossed your cookies.

NANCY
Do you realize how crude that is?

MICHAEL
Listen. We're all decent people. All four of us. How do we get all carried away, losing our tempers? It's entirely unnecessary.

PENELOPE
Oh Michael, stop it! That's enough mitigating. We're only superficially fair-minded, so let's not be fair-minded at all!

MICHAEL
Oh no, I'm not going to be led down that path.

ALAN
What path?

MICHAEL
The path those two little shits led us down! All right?

ALAN
I'm afraid Pen doesn't see things that way.

PENELOPE
Penelope!

ALAN
Sorry.

PENELOPE
So now poor Ethan is a little shit.
That really takes the cake.

ALAN
OK, that's it. I really have to leave now.

NANCY
So do I.

PENELOPE
Go. Go. I give up.
The LONGSTREET family's telephone rings.

MICHAEL
Hello?

MICHAEL'S MOTHER (O.S. - TEL)
It's me, Mikey.

MICHAEL
Oh, hi Ma.

MICHAEL'S MOTHER (O.S. - TEL)
This a bad time?

MICHAEL
No. Well, we got some friends over but go ahead.

MICHAEL'S MOTHER (O.S. - TEL)
You know the surgeon told me to stop taking my medication before the operation.

MICHAEL
Yes, Ma. Do what the doctors tell you to do.

MICHAEL'S MOTHER (O.S. - TEL)
All of them?

MICHAEL
Yes.

MICHAEL'S MOTHER (O.S. - TEL)

Because the surgeon told me to stop all of them but Dr. Perlstein said I could keep taking the Antril?

MICHAEL
The what?

MICHAEL'S MOTHER (O.S. - TEL)
Should I stop the Antril too?

MICHAEL
Antril! You're taking... You're taking Antril?! Wait, wait. Hang on a second, Ma.
(to ALAN:)
Antril? That crap of yours, is that Antril? My mother's taking it!

ALAN
Thousands of people take it.

MICHAEL
(on phone:)
All right, you stop taking that one immediately. You hear me, Ma? Right now.

MICHAEL'S MOTHER (O.S. - TEL)
Why? It's good for my pressure.

MICHAEL
Don't argue. I'll explain later.

MICHAEL'S MOTHER (O.S. - TEL)
Perlstein says I can keep the
Antril.

MICHAEL
You tell Dr. Perlstein that I won't let you.

MICHAEL'S MOTHER (O.S. - TEL)
I ordered the crutches, by the way.

MICHAEL
Good.

MICHAEL'S MOTHER (O.S. - TEL)
Red ones.

MICHAEL
What? Why red?

MICHAEL'S MOTHER (O.S. - TEL)
So they can see me.

MICHAEL
So who can see you?

MICHAEL'S MOTHER (O.S. - TEL)
The cars! They all drive like crazy!

MICHAEL
Mom, that's ridiculous.

MICHAEL'S MOTHER
Doris got run ov-

MICHAEL
All right, we'll talk about it later. We have company, Ma. I'll call you back.
(hangs up)
She got red crutches so she won't get run over by a truck. Just in case, in her condition, she wanders out on the highway in the middle of the night.
They're giving her Antril for her blood pressure.

ALAN
If she's taking it and she looks normal, I'll take her deposition. Didn't I have a scarf? Oh there it is.

MICHAEL
I don't like that attitude of yours. If my mother has the slightest symptom, my name will be at the top of a class-action suit.

ALAN
We'll have one anyway.

MICHAEL
I should hope so!

NANCY
Goodbye, Mrs. Longstreet.

PENELOPE
Doing the right thing is futile. Honesty is just stupidity. All it does is weaken you. You let your guard down.

ALAN
OK, let's go Nancy. That's enough sermons and lectures for one day.
ALAN picks up NANCY's coat and hands it to her, then leads her toward the foyer. Nancy puts her coat on as she crosses the room.

MICHAEL
(taking a step or two after them:)

Go ahead, go. But let me tell you one thing. Now that I know you, I think what's-his-name, Zachary, may have some pretty extenuating circumstances.

NANCY stops and turns half-way toward MICHAEL.

NANCY
When you killed that hamster -

MICHAEL
Killed?!

NANCY
Killed.

MICHAEL
I killed the hamster?!

NANCY
Yes. You do everything you can to make us feel guilty, you stake out the moral highground as your own, but you yourself are a murderer.

MICHAEL
I definitely did not kill that hamster!

NANCY
Worse. You left it out there, trembling with fear in a hostile environment. That poor critter was probably eaten by a dog or a rat.

PENELOPE
She's right about that! She's right about that!

MICHAEL
What do you mean she's right?

PENELOPE
She is. I mean, seriously. It's horrible, what must have happened to that animal!

MICHAEL
I thought the hamster would be happy to be free. I was sure he'd go running around in the gutter, happy as a clam!

PENELOPE
He didn't.

NANCY
And you just left him there.

MICHAEL
I can't touch those things! I can't touch anything of that family. Christ, Penny, you know that!

PENELOPE

He's afraid of rodents.

MICHAEL

Yes, I have a fear of rodents. I'm terrified of reptiles. Anything down close to the ground, no thanks! That's all it is.

ALAN

(to PENELOPE:)

What about you? How come you didn't go downstairs and get it?

PENELOPE

Hey, I didn't even know! Michael told the kids and me, the next morning, that the hamster ran away. I went right out looking for it, I went right out. I went all the way around the block, I went down to the basement.

MICHAEL

Penelope, it is completely unfair that all of a sudden I'm in the hot seat about this hamster thing, that you just had to tell them about. That's a family issue that doesn't concern anybody but us and it's got nothing to do with this situation here! And I can't believe I'm getting called a murderer in my own house!

PENELOPE

What does your house have to do with the price of tea in China?

MICHAEL

It's my house and I open the doors, the doors are wide open in a spirit of reconciliation, to people who should be a little grateful!

ALAN

Keep right on stroking your own ego, it's beautiful.

NANCY

You have no remorse?

MICHAEL

I have no remorse. That animal was disgusting. I'm glad it's gone.

PENELOPE

Michael, that's ridiculous.

MICHAEL

What's ridiculous? What, have you lost your mind, too, now? Their son beats the shit out of Ethan and you're in my face over a hamster?

PENELOPE

What you did with that hamster was wrong, you can't deny that.

MICHAEL
I don't give a fuck about the hamster!

PENELOPE
You'll have to give a fuck tonight when your daughter gets home.

MICHAEL
Bring her on! I'm not going to be told how to act by a nine-year-old snotnose brat!

ALAN
Now I agree with him there, one hundred percent.

PENELOPE
That's pathetic.

MICHAEL
Watch it, Penelope, watch it. I've kept my shirt on up till now, but you're pushing me over a line.

NANCY
And Ethan?

MICHAEL
What about Ethan?

NANCY
Is he sad too?

MICHAEL
Ethan's got other things on his plate, if you ask me.

PENELOPE
Ethan wasn't so attached to Nibbles.

MICHAEL
What kind of pussy name is that anyway?!

NANCY
If you feel no remorse, why should our son?

MICHAEL
You know what? All this consultation and consideration shit, I'm sick to death of it. We were nice to you. We bought tulips. My wife dressed me up as a liberal, but the truth is I got no patience for this touchy-feely bullshit and I'm a temperamental son of a bitch.

ALAN
We all are.

PENELOPE

No. No, I'm sorry. We are not all temperamental sons of bitches.

ALAN
Not you, of course.

PENELOPE
No, not me! Thank heavens!

MICHAEL
Not you, darjee, not you. You're so evolved. You never go off half-cocked.

PENELOPE
Why are you being so aggressive with me?

MICHAEL
I'm not being aggressive. I'm being honest.

PENELOPE
Yes you are aggressive, and you know it.

MICHAEL
You put this little bash together and I let you recruit me...

PENELOPE
You let me recruit you?

MICHAEL
Yes.

PENELOPE
That is so disgusting.

MICHAEL
No, it's not. You're an advocate for civilized behavior, well that's fine with me.

PENELOPE
I'm an advocate for civilized behavior, you bet I am! And it's a good thing somebody is!
(on the verge of tears:)
You think it's better to be a son of a bitch?

ALAN
All right, all right...

PENELOPE
(still about to cry:)
That's OK to criticize someone for not being a temperamental son of a bitch?

NANCY

Nobody said that. Nobody criticized you for that.

PENELOPE
You did!
(she cries)

ALAN
We did not.

PENELOPE
What was I supposed to do? Sue you? Never talk to you and tear you to pieces through the insurance company?

MICHAEL
Stop it, Penny.

PENELOPE
Stop what?!

MICHAEL
You're blowing this all out of proportion.

PENELOPE
I don't care! You do everything you can to avoid the pettiness and you wind up humiliated and completely alone!
ALAN's cell vibrates again.

ALAN
Yes.

WALTER (O.S. - TEL)
It's spreading like wild fire. It's out everywhere.

ALAN
Let them prove it!

WALTER (O.S. - TEL)
Yeah.

ALAN
Prove it!

WALTER (O.S. - TEL)
Without some kind of response...

ALAN
From where I sit, the best thing for us to do is nothing!

MICHAEL

We're born alone and we die alone!
Who wants a little Scotch?

WALTER (O.S. - TEL)
You know I keep going over this in my mind, Alan. The victims -

ALAN
Walter, I'm in a meeting right now. I'll call you when I get back to the office.
He hangs up.

PENELOPE
That's the thing. I am living with a totally negative person.

ALAN
Who's negative?

MICHAEL
Me.

PENELOPE
This was the worst possible idea! We should never have had this meeting at all!

MICHAEL
I told you so.

PENELOPE
You told me so?

MICHAEL
Yeah.

PENELOPE
You told me that you didn't want to have this meeting?!

MICHAEL
I didn't think it was a very good idea.
MICHAEL crosses to the liquor cabinet, pulls out a bottle of scotch.

NANCY
It was a good idea.

MICHAEL
Oh come on!
(holding up the bottle:)
Who wants some?

PENELOPE
You told me it wasn't a good idea,
Michael?!

MICHAEL
As I recall.

PENELOPE
As you recall!

ALAN
Maybe just a sip.

NANCY
Don't you have to go?

ALAN
At this point in the game, I may as well have a drink.
MICHAEL pours two glasses of scotch and hands one to ALAN.

PENELOPE
Look me in the eyes and tell me again we didn't both agree to this!

NANCY
Calm down, Penelope, calm down. This is going nowhere.

PENELOPE
Who said not to touch the cobbler this morning? Who said we should keep the rest for the Cowan's? Who said that?!

ALAN
That was very nice of you.

MICHAEL
What's that got to do with it?

PENELOPE
What do you mean what has it got to do with it?!

MICHAEL
Guests are guests.

PENELOPE
You're lying, you're lying! He's lying!

ALAN
You know my wife actually had to drag me here today. When you grow up with a certain John Wayne idea of manhood, the impulse in this kind of situation is not to talk it through.

MICHAEL
Ha, ha!

NANCY
I thought the role model was Ivanhoe.

ALAN
Same basic concept.

MICHAEL
Another aspect.

PENELOPE
Another aspect! Just how much are you going to humiliate yourself, huh?

NANCY
I can see I dragged him here for nothing.

ALAN
What did you expect, Doodle? That is a ridiculous nickname. Some revelation about universal values? This scotch is unbelievable.

MICHAEL
Ah! See that? 18 years old, single malt, from a tiny place in Scotland where they still grow their own barley.

PENELOPE
And the tulips, who went to get them? All I said was it's too bad we didn't get any tulips. I never said anything about going all the way up to Sullivan at dawn.

NANCY
Don't get all bent out of shape over this, Penelope, it's not worth it.

PENELOPE
He got the tulips! Him and only him!
Don't we get a drink?

NANCY
Penelope and I would like a drink, too.
Pause. Michael crosses to the bar.
Pretty funny when you think about it, a devotee of Ivanhoe and John Wayne but he's scared to pick up an itty-bitty mouse.

MICHAEL
Stop with the hamster! Stop!
MICHAEL serves NANCY some scotch.

PENELOPE
Ha, ha! You're right, it's laughable!

NANCY

And her?

MICHAEL
I don't think that will be necessary.

PENELOPE
Pour me a drink, Michael.

MICHAEL
No.

PENELOPE
Michael!

MICHAEL
No.
PENELOPE tries to tear the bottle away from him.
MICHAEL won't let her.

NANCY
What is wrong with you, Michael?!
MICHAEL hands PENELOPE the bottle.

MICHAEL
Fine, go ahead. Drink, drink, what does it matter?

NANCY
Is drinking bad for you or something?

PENELOPE
It's great for me. At this point...
She pours herself a drink, takes a sip, breaks down crying.

ALAN
Well... Now I don't know...

PENELOPE
(to ALAN:)
Mr. uh...

NANCY
Alan.

PENELOPE
Alan, you and I didn't exactly hit it off but you see, I live with a man who has decided once and for all that life is synonymous with mediocrity. It's very hard to live with a man who's walled himself up in that idea, who doesn't want to change anything, who never gets excited about anything.

MICHAEL

What does he care? He could care less.

PENELOPE

One needs to believe. To believe in some possible correction, right?

MICHAEL

He's the last guy on earth you should be telling all this to.

PENELOPE

I'll talk to anyone I damn well please!
The LONGSTREET family's phone rings.

MICHAEL

Who the fuck is that now?
(reading the caller
ID and picking up:)
Yes, Ma.

MICHAEL'S MOTHER (O.S. - TEL)

Mikey, it's me again. I forgot to ask, how is Ethan?

MICHAEL

He's fine. Well I mean he got his teeth knocked out but he's fine.

MICHAEL'S MOTHER (O.S. - TEL)

He's in pain?

MICHAEL

He's in pain. It hurts, it'll pass.
Ma, I'm busy. I'll call you back.
He hangs up.

NANCY

He's still in pain?

PENELOPE

No.

NANCY

Then why do you worry your mother?

PENELOPE

He can't help himself. He always has to worry her.

MICHAEL

OK, that's enough Penelope! What is this drama queen bullshit?

ALAN

Penelope, nobody cares about anything outside himself. Sure, we'd all like to believe in some kind of possible correction, one we could author ourselves, completely free of selfish consideration. Like you're writing this book about Darfur, and that's great. I understand how you might say, OK, I'll pick a massacre, history is full of them, and I'm going to write a book. Everybody has to save himself somehow.

PENELOPE
I'm not writing this book to save myself. You haven't read it, you don't know what's in it.

ALAN
Whatever.

PENELOPE
That smell of Kronos is killing me!

MICHAEL
It reeks!

ALAN
You didn't exactly skimp.

NANCY
I'm so sorry.

PENELOPE
It's not your fault. I'm the one who sprayed like a madwoman. And why can't we just take it easy once in a while? Why does everything always have to be so exhausting?

ALAN
You think too much. Women think too much.

NANCY
(sarcastic:)
There's an original response!
(to Penelope:)
Which must be pleasantly disconcerting to you.

PENELOPE
I don't know what that means, to think too much. And I don't understand how you can go on living without some moral sense of the world.

MICHAEL
Look at me, I'm living!

PENELOPE
Shut up! I detest that miserable complicity of yours! You disgust me!

MICHAEL

What happened to your sense of humor?

PENELOPE
I don't have a sense of humor. And I don't want one.

MICHAEL
If you ask me, the couple is the most terrible ordeal God ever inflicted on us.

NANCY
Marvelous.

MICHAEL
The couple and the family.

NANCY
No one's forcing you to air this out in front of us, Michael. And I might add, it's a little indecent.

PENELOPE
That doesn't bother him.

MICHAEL
Don't you agree?

NANCY
This is all off point. Alan, say something.

ALAN
He has a right to his ideas.

NANCY
That doesn't mean he has to advertise them.

ALAN
Yeah, all right, maybe...

NANCY
We don't care about their marriage. We're here about a problem with the kids. We don't care about their marriage.

ALAN
Yeah, except...

NANCY
Except what? What are you saying?

ALAN
It is related.

MICHAEL
It's related! Of course it's related!

PENELOPE
Ethan's getting two of his teeth broken is related to our marriage?!

MICHAEL
Of course it is.

NANCY
We don't follow you.

MICHAEL
Take a step back and look at the situation we're in. Children suck the life out of you and leave us old and empty. It's the law of nature.
(MORE)

MICHAEL (CONT'D)
You see these young couples, laughing all the way to the altar, and you think they don't know. Poor fuckers don't know a thing. They're happy. Nobody briefs you in the beginning. This army buddy of mine is going to have a kid with his new girlfriend. I say to him, a kid at our age, what are you stupid? You got ten, fifteen good years left before you get cancer or have a stroke and you're going to saddle yourself with a fucking kid?

NANCY
That's not really what you think.

PENELOPE
Yes it is.

MICHAEL
Of course it's what I think. Look, I think even worse.

PENELOPE
Yeah.

NANCY
You're debasing yourself, Michael.

MICHAEL
Is that right? Ha, ha!

NANCY
Stop crying, Penelope. It only makes it worse.
ALAN hands him his empty glass. MICHAEL refills it.

MICHAEL
Of course, of course. Excellent, isn't it?

ALAN
Excellent.

MICHAEL
Could I interest you in a cigar?

PENELOPE
No! No cigars here!

ALAN
Too bad.

NANCY
Were you going to smoke a cigar now,
Alan?

ALAN
I do what I want, Nancy. If I want to smoke a cigar, I smoke a cigar. I won't smoke it because
I don't want to upset Penelope who's already on edge, to put it mildly.
(to PENELOPE:)
She's right, quit snuffling like that. When women cry, men are pushed to a breaking point.
Although unfortunately, I must say that Michael's point of view is completely justified.
The cell phone vibrates.

ALAN (CONT'D)
Yes, Dennis.

DENNIS (O.S. - TEL)
Can I read it to you?

ALAN
Go ahead.

DENNIS (O.S. - TEL)
TW Pharma Corporation...

ALAN
Put New York, and a specific time of day.

NANCY
It's unbearable!
ALAN moves away a little and keeps his voice down, to escape NANCY's ire.

DENNIS (O.S. - TEL)
What time of day?

ALAN
The time you send it. It has to be hot off the press.

DENNIS (O.S. - TEL)
TW Pharma Corporation questions...

ALAN
No, not "questions". "Deplores".
Questions is wishy-washy.

NANCY
I live with this night and day! He's glued to his cell phone! Our lives are chopped up by the cell phone.

ALAN
Uh... One second.
(covering the phone:)
Nancy, this is very important.

NANCY
It's always very important. What's happening somewhere else is always more important.

ALAN
(back to call:)
Go ahead.

DENNIS (O.S. - TEL)
...deliberately deceitful allegations...

ALAN
Yeah.

DENNIS (O.S. - TEL)
...forming part of a strategy two weeks from the company's posting...

ALAN
Not "strategy". "Scheme". A scheme surfacing two weeks from the company's posting, etcetera.

NANCY
In the street. At the dinner table.
Everywhere.

DENNIS (O.S. - TEL)
The company has serious doubts about the source and funding of this study coming as it does...

ALAN
"A study" in quotes. Put the word "study" in quotes.
Dennis continues reading the press release on phone, but only portions of what he says are audible.

NANCY
I don't even protest anymore.
Unconditional surrender. I feel like
I'm going to vomit again.

MICHAEL
Where's that bucket?

PENELOPE
I don't know.

DENNIS (O.S. - TEL)
At the eve of the annual stockholder's meeting. This may indeed be a barefaced attempt at manipulating the stock price and damage TW Pharma's reputation. Now Walter thinks that line is a little dicy.

ALAN
Then just quote me. "This is a barefaced attempt to manipulate the stock price..."

PENELOPE
It's over there. Go stand near it, please.

MICHAEL
Pen.

PENELOPE
It's all right. We're set up to handle this now.

ALAN
"...the stock price and destabilize my client," according to TW Pharma attorney Alan Cowan.

DENNIS (O.S. - TEL)
OK, I'll make these corrections and we'll put it out there.

ALAN
AP, Reuters, major newspapers, trade journals, the whole shebang.
He hangs up.

ALAN (CONT'D)
What is wrong with you?!

MICHAEL
She's going to throw up again.

NANCY
You're so caring, it's touching.

ALAN

I'm worried!

NANCY
I didn't get that. My mistake.

ALAN
Oh come on Nancy, will you! You and I don't have to do this.
(MORE)

ALAN (CONT'D)
Their marriage is going downhill, we don't have to try to compete with them!

PENELOPE
What gives you the right to say our marriage is going downhill? What gives you the right?
ALAN's cell vibrates again.

ALAN
Walter.

WALTER (O.S. - TEL)
Is the press release ready, Alan?

ALAN
I just had it read back. They're sending it over to you.

WALTER (O.S. - TEL)
And you do say this is an attempt at...

ALAN
Manipulation. Manipulation of the stock price. I'll call you right back.
(hangs up)
I didn't say it. Steven did.

PENELOPE
Michael.

ALAN
Michael, sorry.

PENELOPE
I won't let you judge our family.

ALAN
Then don't judge our son either.

PENELOPE
That's different! Your son brutalized our son!

ALAN

They're young, they're just kids. Kids roughhouse in the playground, always have always will. It's a rule of nature.

PENELOPE
No! No it isn't!

ALAN
Sure it is. It takes a little education to substitute the rule of law for violence. The origin of law, of course you know, is brute force.

PENELOPE
Maybe for cavemen it was. Not in this world.

ALAN
In this world? Tell me about this world.

PENELOPE
You're boring. This whole conversation is boring.

ALAN
Penelope, I believe in the god of carnage. The god whose rule has been unchallenged since time immemorial. You're interested in Africa, right?
NANCY is retching.

ALAN (CONT'D)
What's the matter?

NANCY
Don't worry about me.

ALAN
Nancy.

NANCY
I'm just fine.

ALAN
See, I just got back from the Congo. They got kids there, trained to kill at the age of eight. In the course of their childhood, they might kill hundreds of people. They'll kill with a machete, a shotgun, a Kalash, a thumper. So obviously when my son busts some other kid's tooth, even two teeth, with a bamboo switch by the sandbox, I'm not quite as shocked and indignant as you are.

PENELOPE
Well you should be.

NANCY
(exaggerating the military sound of the jargon:)
Thumper!

ALAN
Yes, that's what they call a grenade launcher.
NANCY spits into the pail.

MICHAEL
You all right?

NANCY
I'm just fine.

ALAN
What the hell is wrong with you?
What's wrong with her?

NANCY
It's bile. It's nothing.

PENELOPE
Don't tell me about Africa. I know all about suffering in Africa.

ALAN
I don't doubt it.

PENELOPE
That's all I've been thinking about for months...

MICHAEL
Don't get her started with this!
Please!
PENELOPE charges her husband and strikes him, several times, wild with despair and irrational abandon.
ALAN pulls her off.

ALAN
You know I'm actually starting to like you.

PENELOPE
Shut up!

MICHAEL
Talk about commitment to world peace and stability.

PENELOPE
Shut the fuck up, Michael!
NANCY wretches again.
She takes her glass of scotch and brings it to her lips.

MICHAEL

You sure about that?

NANCY
Very sure. This will do me some good.

PENELOPE
We live in New York City. We don't live in Kinshasa! We live in New York, with the customs of western society. What happens in a Brooklyn playground is about western values! To which, like it or not, I happen to subscribe!

MICHAEL
Beating your husband must be one of those customs then...

PENELOPE
Michael, I am warning you.

ALAN
She was all over you like a bad rash!
If I were you it would melt my heart.

PENELOPE
I might finish the job soon.

NANCY
He's making fun of you, do you believe it?

PENELOPE
I don't give a shit about him.

ALAN
No, really. Morally, we're supposed to overcome our impulses but there are times you don't want to overcome them. I mean, who wants to say a Hail Mary when you're having sex? Can you buy this scotch around here?

MICHAEL
This stuff, not very likely!

NANCY
Thumper! Ha, ha!

PENELOPE
Thumper, really!

ALAN
Yes. Thumper.

NANCY
Why don't you just say grenade launcher?

ALAN
Because that's the term. Just like they say "kalash" and not Kalashnikov or AK-47.

NANCY
Who is they?

ALAN
That's enough, Nancy. That's enough.

NANCY
Hotshot firebrands like my husband, you got to understand, it's hard for them to get excited about what happens down the block.

ALAN
Exactly.

PENELOPE
I don't see why. I don't see why. We're all citizens of the world. I don't see why we shouldn't have some sense of community.

MICHAEL
Oh Penny! Give us a break with the highfalutin clap trap!

PENELOPE
I'm going to kill him.
The cell vibrates.

ALAN
Yes.

DENNIS (O.S. - TEL)
We read it to him. He has a problem with "barefaced".

ALAN
So take out "barefaced".

DENNIS (O.S. - TEL)
What should we..?

ALAN
"Brazen". A brazen attempt to...

DENNIS (O.S. - TEL)
Manipulate the stock price.

ALAN
There you go.

PENELOPE

She's right, it's unbearable after a while.

ALAN
He signed off on the rest?

DENNIS (O.S. - TEL)
Yeah.

ALAN
Good. That's fine.
(hangs up)
What were we talking about? Thumpers?

PENELOPE
I was saying that, whatever my husband thinks, whether it happens here or thousands of miles away, we must be equally concerned.

ALAN
Equally concerned... Yeah... Nancy, it's absurd to drink in your condition.

NANCY
What condition? I'm perfect.

ALAN
It's an interesting idea...
(picks up cell)
Yes.

DENNIS (O.S. - TEL)
We're saying nothing before the release, right? Interviews?

ALAN
No, no interviews before we get this release out.

DENNIS (O.S. - TEL)
He wants to appear humane. He thinks the stockholders may be sensitive to an expression...

PENELOPE
Mr. Cowan, would you please put an end to this nerve-racking conversation?!

ALAN
(on phone:)
No way. The stockholders won't give a shit. Just remind him that...
NANCY walks to ALAN, tears his cell phone away and, after briefly looking around for where to put it, dunks it in the tulip vase.

ALAN (CONT'D)
Nancy, what are you..!!

NANCY
There.

PENELOPE
Ha, ha! Way to go!

MICHAEL
(horrified:)
Oh my god!

ALAN
Are you out of your fucking mind?
Shit!!
He rushes to the vase. MICHAEL, who has gotten there first, fishes the phone out. It's soaking wet.

MICHAEL
The blow-dryer! Where's the blow- dryer?!
He finds it and plugs it back into the socket. He immediately turns it on and points it at the cell phone.
Because of the short wire, he has to stay close to the wall.

ALAN
You should be put in a home, dear! I can't believe this! I got everything in there. It's brand new, I spent hours setting it up!
MICHAEL speaks to NANCY, over the loud noise of the blow dryer:

MICHAEL
I can't believe you did that. That was an irresponsible thing to do.

ALAN
I got everything, my whole life was in there.

NANCY
His whole life!
She downs her glass of scotch. The noise continues.

MICHAEL
Hang on, maybe we'll get it running again.

ALAN
No way. It's history!

MICHAEL
I want to take out the battery and the SIM card. How do you open it?
ALAN tries, but he has no idea.

ALAN
I just got it, I don't know.

MICHAEL
Let me see.

ALAN
And they think it's funny, they think it's funny!
MICHAEL puts the blow dryer down without turning it off.
He hunkers down by the wall and easily opens the cell phone. Then he lays out the various elements on the floor in a line.

MICHAEL
There.
He picks up the blow dryer and goes back to work. PENELOPE laughs heartily.

MICHAEL (CONT'D)
Penelope, this is not funny!

PENELOPE
My husband has spent the entire afternoon drying things!

NANCY
Ha, ha, ha!
NANCY goes right ahead and pours herself another glass of scotch.
MICHAEL, who doesn't see any humor in it, is working very dilligently. ALAN has slid down on to the ground next to him, back to the wall.
The cell phone parts - battery, SIM card, cover, all tremble in the warm breeze from the blow dryer. The lighter pieces even move slightly.
MICHAEL puts them back in order.
For a moment, the only sound is that of the blow-dryer.
ALAN is completely demoralized.
They look like a couple of sad-eyed children, only one of whom is still trying to have fun.

ALAN
Forget it, man. Forget it. Nothing can be done.
MICHAEL finally turns off the blow-dryer.

MICHAEL
Got to wait.
(after an awkward silence:)
You want to use the phone?
ALAN shakes his head no, shrugs to say he doesn't care.

MICHAEL (CONT'D)
I must say...

NANCY
What must you say, Michael?

MICHAEL

No. I don't even know what to say.

NANCY
I'd say it feels better. It feels better like this.
(beat)
I'd say it's more peaceful, wouldn't you? Men get so attached to their toys. It diminishes them. They lose their credibility. A man should have both hands free... In my opinion. Even briefcases. I liked this guy once and then I saw him carrying this rectangular bag, with a shoulder strap. A man's bag, but with a shoulder strap. It was over. A bag with a shoulder strap, that's the worst. But the cell phone always at his fingertips is the worst, too. A man should seem alone. In my opinion. Seem like he can go it alone. I've got a John Wayne idea of manhood, too. What was it he had? A Colt '45. Something that empties a room... Any man that doesn't give off those loner vibes just doesn't come off as having any substance... So Michael I guess you're happy now.
(MORE)

NANCY (CONT'D)
Our touchy-feely - whatever you said - is coming apart at the seams. But hey, you know what? This almost feels good. In my opinion.

MICHAEL
Yeah, well in my opinion, some people can hold their liquor better than others.

NANCY
I'm as normal as can be.

MICHAEL
Yeah, right.

NANCY
I'm beginning to see things with a pleasant serenity.

PENELOPE
Ha, ha! That's so good! A pleasant serenity!

MICHAEL
I can't understand why you're wasting yourself, right out in the open, darjeeling.

PENELOPE
Shut the hell up.
MICHAEL gets up and takes a box of cigars from a corner cabinet. He comes back and holds it out to ALAN.

MICHAEL
Take one, Alan. Relax.

PENELOPE
No cigar smoke in the house!

MICHAEL
Hoyo de Monterrey, or Partagas D number 4. You got your Hoyo
Coronation or Epicure number 2.

ALAN
Where did you get these?

MICHAEL
You don't want to know.

ALAN
Seriously.

MICHAEL
The Spanish connection.

Alan knits his brow.

MICHAEL (CONT'D)
My cookware guy. His best friend is going with a flight attendant.
Brings in like two boxes a week.

PENELOPE
You can't smoke in a house with an asthmatic child! And stop telling him your whole life
story.

NANCY
Who has asthma?

PENELOPE
Our son.

MICHAEL
We had a goddamn hamster, didn't we?

NANCY
It's true that pets aren't good when you're asthmatic.

MICHAEL
Not good at all!

NANCY
Even goldfish aren't necessarily recommended.

PENELOPE
Do I have to listen to this crap?
PENELOPE tears the cigar box away from MICHAEL and slams it shut.

PENELOPE (CONT'D)

I'm sorry, I guess I'm the only one who doesn't see things with pleasant serenity. To tell you the truth, I've never been so unhappy. I think this is the unhappiest day of my whole life.

MICHAEL
You're an unhappy drunk.

PENELOPE
Michael, every word out of your mouth just slays me. I don't get drunk. I had a sip of your shitty eighteen-year old single malt... that you trot out like it's the eighth wonder of the world. I don't get drunk, and believe me I wish I could.
(MORE)

PENELOPE (CONT'D)
It would be such a relief to drown every little sorrow in a good stiff drink.

NANCY
My husband is unhappy, too. Look at him. All hunched over. Like he was left on the side of the road. I think this is the unhappiest day of his life, too.

ALAN
It is.

NANCY
I'm sorry, Doodle.
MICHAEL hits the cell phone parts with the blow-dryer again.

PENELOPE
Turn that blow-dryer off! His thing is a goner.
The LONGSTREET family's phone rings.

PENELOPE (CONT'D)
(re: the phone)
Michael. Michael!
MICHAEL turns off the blow dryer, picks up the phone.

MICHAEL
Yeah!

MICHAEL'S MOTHER (O.S. - TEL)
Mikey.

MICHAEL
Mom, I told you we're busy here.

MICHAEL'S MOTHER (O.S. - TEL)
Why do you want me to stop taking my Antril?

MICHAEL

Because it's medication that can kill you! It's poison!

MICHAEL'S MOTHER (O.S. - TEL)
It is not. It's...

MICHAEL
Here, there's someone here who can explain.
He hands the phone to ALAN.

MICHAEL (CONT'D)
Tell her.

ALAN
Tell her what?

MICHAEL
Tell her what you know about that deadly shit of yours.

NANCY
What can he tell her? He doesn't know anything!

MICHAEL'S MOTHER
Mikey? Hello.

ALAN
Hello? How are you feeling ma'am?

MICHAEL'S MOTHER (O.S. - TEL)
I'm all right for now but they want to take me off my medicine.

ALAN
Yes.

MICHAEL'S MOTHER (O.S. - TEL)
My operation is a week away.

ALAN
And are you in pain?

MICHAEL'S MOTHER (O.S. - TEL)
I can't be on my feet, Doctor.

ALAN
Of course. But the operation will fix that.

MICHAEL'S MOTHER (O.S. - TEL)
The worst part is, they have to do the other leg later.

ALAN
The other leg too, huh?

MICHAEL'S MOTHER (O.S. - TEL)
Are you an orthopedist?

ALAN
No, I'm not an orthopedist.
(aside:)
She keeps calling me doctor.

NANCY
Doctor, what a laugh! Hang up!

MICHAEL'S MOTHER (O.S. - TEL)
Hello? What is all this about my
Antril?

ALAN
But you're... I mean, you don't have any balance issues?

MICHAEL'S MOTHER (O.S. - TEL)
No, I just drag my foot a little. Can it kill me, Doctor? Can it really kill me?

ALAN
No, of course not. Not at all. Don't listen to what people say. Still, it's probably a good idea for you not to take it anymore for a while.

MICHAEL'S MOTHER (O.S. - TEL)
For how long?

ALAN
Just until... Until this operation is behind you.

MICHAEL'S MOTHER (O.S. - TEL)
They're going to ruin me. If you could see me, you'd be surprised how well preserved I am!

ALAN
Yes, sounds like you're in excellent shape.
MICHAEL tears the phone away.

MICHAEL
All right, Ma. You got that? Stop taking that medication. Just stop taking it, do as you're told. I'll call you back.
(hangs up)
I can't take her anymore. The shit you put up with in life!

NANCY

All right, should we wrap this up? Should I come back tonight with Zachary? Let's decide. This is getting to be like, who cares? That is what we're here for, after all.

PENELOPE
Now I'm going to be sick. Where's the bucket?
MICHAEL takes the bottle of scotch and puts it out of NANCY's reach.

MICHAEL
That's enough.

NANCY
I'd say both sides share the blame. So there you are. Both sides share the blame.

PENELOPE
What, you're serious?

NANCY
Excuse me?

PENELOPE
Is that what you really think?

NANCY
It's what I think, yes.

PENELOPE
Our son Ethan, who took codeine last night at three in the morning, shares the blame?

NANCY
He's not necessarily innocent.

PENELOPE
Get the fuck out! Get out of my house.
She grabs NANCY's handbag and throws it against the door.
All the contents spill out.

PENELOPE (CONT'D)
Get the fuck out!

NANCY
My bag!
(like a little girl:)
Alan!

MICHAEL
What is going on here? They've totally lost it.
NANCY picks up the items that have fallen from her bag.

NANCY

Alan, do something!

PENELOPE
"Alan, do something!"

NANCY
Shut your mouth! She broke my make-up mirror! And my perfume!
(to ALAN:)
Stand up for me. Why don't you stand up for me?

ALAN
Let's go.
He starts picking up the pieces of his cell phone.

PENELOPE
It's not like I'm strangling her!

NANCY
What did I do to you?!

PENELOPE
The blame is not shared! The victim and the criminal are not the same!

NANCY
The criminal!

MICHAEL
Oh give it a fucking rest, Penelope!
Enough of these idealistic theories!

PENELOPE
Which I believe in.

MICHAEL
Yeah, you believe, you believe. This crush you got on these Sudan sambos is spilling over into everything now!

PENELOPE
I am horrified. How can you be so openly despicable?

MICHAEL
Because I feel like it. I feel like being openly despicable.

PENELOPE
One day you'll understand the sheer horror of what's happening in that part of the world and you'll be ashamed of your inability to take action, of your contemptibly nihilistic attitude.

MICHAEL
Yes, darjeeling, you're so wonderful! You are the best and the brightest among us!

PENELOPE
Yes. Yes I am.

NANCY
Let's get out of here, Alan. These people are monsters!
NANCY drinks down the rest of her scotch and goes for the bottle. ALAN stops her.

ALAN
Stop it, Nancy.

NANCY
No, I want to drink some more. I want to get drunk off my ass. This bitch throws my bag against a wall and nobody lifts a finger. I want to be blind drunk!

ALAN
You're drunk enough.

NANCY
How can you let her call our son a criminal? We come to their house to work things out with them and they insult us, browbeat us, they lecture us about being good citizens of the planet. I'm glad our son kicked the shit out of your son and I wipe my ass with your human rights!

MICHAEL
A little booze and wow! We see her true self. What happened to that gracious, demure woman with the soft eyes...

PENELOPE
I told you! I told you!

ALAN
What did you tell him?

PENELOPE
That she was fake. This woman is totally fake. I'm sorry.

NANCY
(in distress:)
Ha, ha, ha!

ALAN
When exactly did you say that?

PENELOPE
When you were in the bathroom.

ALAN
You had known her fifteen minutes and you already knew she was fake?

PENELOPE
I pick up on these things in people pretty quickly.

MICHAEL
She does.

PENELOPE
I just have a nose for it.

ALAN
Fake, what does that mean?

NANCY
I don't want to listen to this! Why do you put me through this, Alan!?

ALAN
Relax, Doodle.

PENELOPE
She's a complete phony. She doesn't care any more than you do.

MICHAEL
It's true.

ALAN
It's true.

PENELOPE
It's true! You're saying it's true?

MICHAEL
They don't give a shit! It's so obvious, right from the beginning, they don't give a shit! She doesn't give a shit either, you're right!

ALAN
Like you do?

NANCY
I...

ALAN
(to NANCY:)
Let him talk, honey.
(to MICHAEL:)
Explain to me, Michael, exactly how you care. What does that mean anyway? You're more credible when you're being openly despicable. Truth is, nobody here cares.
(MORE)

ALAN (CONT'D)
Except maybe Penelope, one must acknowledge her integrity.

PENELOPE
I don't need your acknowledgment! I don't need your acknowledgment!

NANCY
But I do care. I really do care.

ALAN
We care in a hysterical way, Nancy. Not like heroic figures of a social movement.
(to PENELOPE:)
I saw your friend Jane Fonda on TV the other day. Made me want to run out and buy a Ku Klux Klan poster.

PENELOPE
My friend Jane Fonda? What the hell does she have to do with this?!

ALAN
You're the same breed. You're the same kind of involved, problem-solver woman. Those are not the women we like, the women we like are sensual, crazy, shot full of hormones. The ones who want to show off how perceptive they are, the gatekeepers of the world, they're a huge turnoff. Even poor Michael, your own husband is turned off...

MICHAEL
Don't you speak for me!

PENELOPE
We don't give a shit about what you like in a woman! Where do you get off spouting these opinions? You're one man whose opinions we don't give a shit about!

ALAN
She's screaming. A quartermaster on a slave ship!

PENELOPE
What about her? She doesn't scream? She didn't just scream that your little asshole was right to beat up ours?

NANCY
He was right! At least our kid isn't a little wimpy-ass faggot!

PENELOPE
Yours is a snitch, that's supposed to be better?

NANCY
(picking up her coat:)
Let's go Alan! Why are we still in this house?

PENELOPE

85

Good question.

She starts toward the door but then crosses back to the tulips and whacks them with her handbag.

The flowers go flying all over the place, in pieces.

NANCY

Here! Here! This is what I think of your stupid flowers, your hideous tulips! Ha, ha, ha!

She breaks down crying.

NANCY (CONT'D)

This is the worst day of my life, too.

Silence.

A long moment of stupor.

ALAN's cell phone, on the coffee table, begins to vibrate and turn.

EXT. PARK AND PLAYGROUND - DAY

At the foot of an oak tree, CLOSE on a hamster.

He is shaking himself out on the ground, where leaves and roots from the tree are all tangled together. The very happy hamster nibbles on an acorn.

WE MOVE UP revealing the same playground as the opening scene of the film.

In the distance, the same group of children who had been in the fight.

They are all playing together happily.

END

Made in the USA
Las Vegas, NV
03 April 2021